W9-ARA-226

Manatee Calves

by Ruth Owen

Consultants:
Dr. Katie Tripp, Director of Science and Conservation
Courtney Edwards, Biologist
www.savethemanatee.org
Maitland, Florida

New York, New York

Credits

Cover and Title Page, © Carol Grant/Flickr Select/Getty images; 4–5, © Carol Grant; 6, © 33Karen33/istockphoto; 7, © Masa Ushioda/seapics.com; 8, © Cosmographics; 9, © Norbert Wu/Minden Pictures/FLPA; 10–11, © Carol Grant; 13T, © D. R. Schrichte/seapics.com; 13B, © D. R. Schrichte/seapics.com; 14–15, © Doug Perrine/seapics.com; 16–17, © Doug Perrine/seapics.com; 17B, © Masa Ushioda/seapics.com; 19, © Carol Grant; 21, © Carol Grant; 22T, © Masa Ushioda/seapics.com; 22C, © Jeff Mondragon/Alamy; 22B, © 33Karen33/istockphoto; 23T, © Doug Perrine/seapics.com; 23B, © D. R. Schrichte/seapics.com.

Publisher: Kenn Goin
Senior Editor: Lisa Wiseman
Creative Director: Spencer Brinker
Design: Emma Randall
Editor: Mark J Sachner
Photo Researcher: Ruby Tuesday Books Ltd

Library of Congress Cataloging-in-Publication Data

Owen, Ruth, 1967–
Manatee calves — (Water babies)
Includes bibliographical references and index.
ISBN 978-1-61772-599-9 (library binding : alk. paper) — ISBN 1-61772-599-4 (library binding : alk. paper)
1. Manatees—Infancy—Juvenile literature. I. Title.
QL737.S63O94 2013
599.55'1392—dc23
2012020366

For more information, write to Bearport Publishing Company, Inc., 45 West 21st Street, Suite 3B, New York, New York 10010. Printed in the United States of America.

10 9 8 7 6 5 4 3 2 1

Contents

Meet a manatee calf

A large, gray animal swims slowly through the water.

It's a West Indian manatee looking for plants to eat.

The manatee is not alone.

Swimming close to her is her little **calf**.

What is a manatee?

A manatee is a large animal that lives in water.

An adult manatee can weigh as much as 1,000 pounds (454 kg).

Sometimes a manatee's back may look green.

This is because it has small, living things called **algae** growing on its skin.

Where do manatees live?

West Indian manatees live in warm ocean waters.

They stay close to the shore where the water is not very deep.

They also spend time in rivers that have slow-moving water.

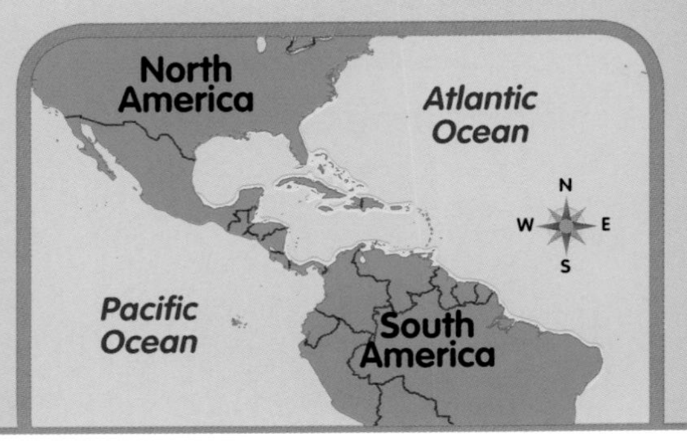

Where West Indian manatees live

river
manatee

A newborn manatee

A manatee mother usually gives birth to just one calf at a time.

The baby manatee is born underwater.

As soon as the calf leaves its mother's body, it swims up to the water's surface.

Here, it takes in its first breath of air.

newborn calf
mother manatee

Water mammals

A newborn manatee needs to breathe air because it is a **mammal**.

Although manatees spend their lives in rivers and oceans, they cannot breathe underwater.

Every three to five minutes, a calf and its mother come to the surface.

They take in some air through their **nostrils**.

Then they sink below the water again.

calf breathing
mother manatee
nostril

Drinking milk

Until it is one or two years old, a manatee calf drinks milk from its mother's body.

The milk comes from a place just behind each of the mother's **flippers**.

Manatee food

Manatees eat underwater grasses and other plants.

A manatee calf first tries these foods when it is a few months old.

By the time it is about one year old, its main food is underwater plants.

It still drinks its mother's milk, however.

A manatee calf's day

A manatee calf spends its day eating and swimming with its mother.

As they swim, the mother and calf make squeaks and whistling sounds.

These sounds are how manatees talk to each other.

mother manatee
a manatee calf exploring

Growing up

When a calf is about two years old, it is ready to leave its mother.

The young manatee goes off on its own.

A male manatee becomes an adult when he is about ten years old.

A female manatee is grown-up at three to five years old.

Once a female manatee is an adult, she is ready to have a calf of her own!

adult manatee

Glossary

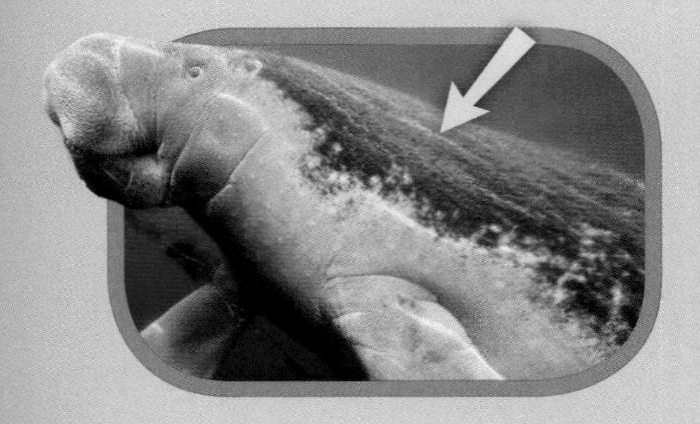

algae (AL-gee) plant-like living things that grow in lakes, ponds, rivers, and oceans

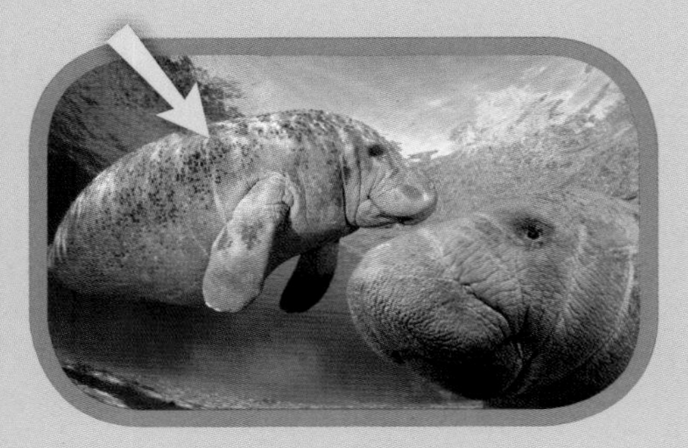

calf (KAF) the baby of an animal such as a manatee or a whale

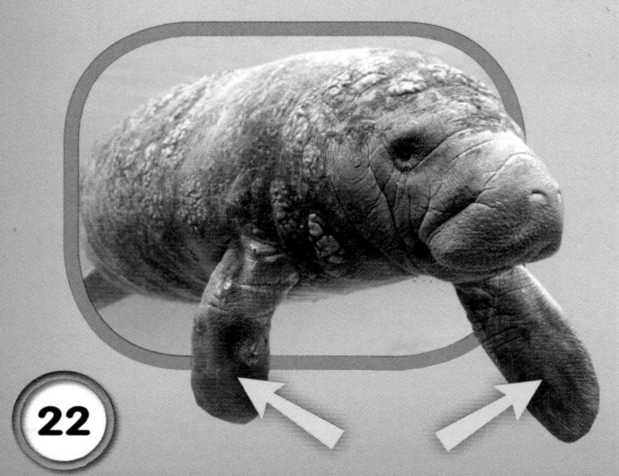

flippers (FLIP-urz) body parts, a little like legs or arms, that water animals such as manatees and dolphins use to help them swim

mammal (MAM-uhl) a warm-blooded animal that usually has fur or hair; most mammals give birth to live babies and feed them milk from their bodies

nostrils (NOSS-truhlz) two openings in the nose that are used for breathing and smelling

Index

Read more

Arnosky, Jim. *All About Manatees. New York: Scholastic (2008).*

Martin, Patricia A. Fink. *Manatees (True Books: Animals).* New York: Scholastic (2002).

Sweeney, Gregory, and Karen Keberle. *Manatees: The Gentle Giants.* Bokeelia, FL: Cuttlefish (2005).

Learn more online

To learn more about manatees, visit **www.bearportpublishing.com/WaterBabies**

About the author

Ruth Owen has been writing children's books for more than ten years. She particularly enjoys working on books about animals and the natural world. Ruth lives in Cornwall, England, just minutes from the ocean. She loves gardening and caring for her family of llamas.